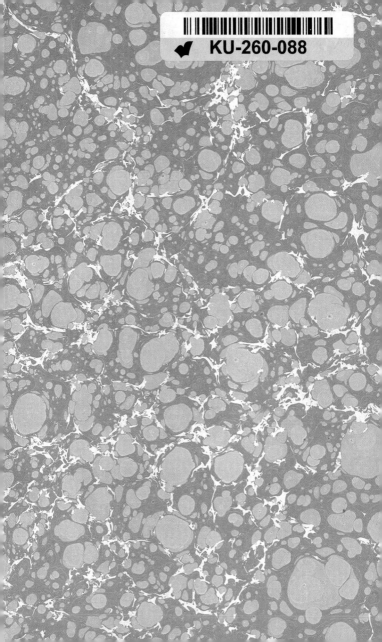

THE ILLUSTRATED POETS

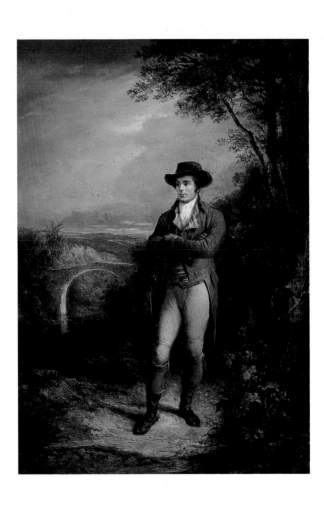

THE ILLUSTRATED POETS

Robert Burns

Selected and with an introduction
by Peter Porter

AURUM PRESS

First published 1992 by Aurum Press Limited,
10 Museum Street, London WC1A 1JS
Selection and introduction copyright © 1992 by Peter Porter

A CIP catalogue record for this book is available from
the British Library.

ISBN 1 85410 225 7

1   3   5   7   9   10   8   6   4   2
1993   1995   1996   1994   1992

Picture research by Juliet Brightmore

Typeset by Computerset
Printed in Hong Kong by Imago

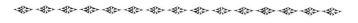

CONTENTS

INTRODUCTION

Robert Burns is a very modern poet in two important ways. His attitudes seem democratic to us ('Man's inhumanity to man …'), though to make his way in the reactionary years at the end of the eighteenth century in Britain he had to compromise his criticism of the class system and his romantic Jacobite sympathies; and he exhibits that duality of character which has become so marked in poets since Romanticism and Modernism – namely, he wrote one way and lived another.

This second claim may seem odd to anyone brought up on the legend of Burns the 'ploughman poet' or, less politely, 'Rab the Ranter' (his slightly gamey name for himself). This is the Burns of generations of sentimental Scots exiles reciting his more tearful and convivial poems on 'Burns Night' and the hero of novels such as *The Wind that Shakes the Barley* – a peasant poet dedicated to whisky, liberty and the love of lasses, condescended to by educated Edinburgh society and killed off by neglect and misunderstanding.

All such legends have some truth in them and there is confirmation of Burns the reveller in his verse – indeed, few poets in our literature can be more genuinely high-spirited or work more happily in the vernacular. This is particularly true of his discursive social poems, such as 'To a Mouse', 'Address to a Haggis' or 'On the Late Captain Gross's Peregrinations'. Although usually written in Lowland Scots (more accurately the dialect of Ayrshire and Dumfries), such poems are firmly in the English Augustan epistolary tradition. They are witty, argumentative, often fantastical, caring more for feats of clever versification

than for lyricism or musical effect. There is nothing barbarous about their poetry: they show Burns to be sophisticated and worldly, an educated poet in the vein of Swift and Pope.

Burns may have been an autodidact and only lightly schooled formally, but he acquired his skill in the places where it counts – by studying and imitating the Scots poets of his day and those of the powerful mainstream tradition outside Scotland. It is one of the wonders of literature how soon, after first committing what he called 'the sin of Rhyme', Burns was producing perfectly crafted original poems filled with his inimitable voice and free from both the stiffness of study and the pains of apprenticeship. His handling of what has come to be called the 'Burns stanza' – four four-foot lines and two two-foot ones with only two rhymes in each stanza – is virtuosic; in his hands it becomes the perfect vehicle for satire, argument and the recording of local detail. He is equally skilled at other forms and can move in and out of Scots and standard English without embarrassment. Burns is, in every sense, a natural or born poet. The duality mentioned earlier lies in the contrast between his totally professional approach to his poetry and the hard, backbreaking toil of his life as an unsuccessful farmer.

After a brilliant start, Burns's career faltered. He was not lionized for long in Edinburgh, and hard work and drinking undermined his health from 1790 onwards. But his contract with the Edinburgh publisher James Johnson led to the production of some of his most important work. He began to write songs or, more properly, to collate and bring to a more perfect state traditional Scots melodies. It is this harvest of song which has made him so loved among Scottish people. As Scotland's national bard, he

sums up the whole of its culture. 'A red, red rose', 'Comin thro the rye', 'The Banks o' Doon' and 'O whistle and I'll come to ye, my lad' show Burns the lyricist at his best. His songs are usually surprisingly direct; though love is depicted as romantic and obsessional, it can be highly realistic as well, as in 'I'm o'er young to marry yet', a brief and brilliant insight into sexual customs among the poor.

Robert Burns was born in 1759 at Alloway near Ayr and grew up on his father's leasehold farm. He received a spasmodic education and began writing poetry early. His first collection of poems was published in 1786; this was the time of his dispute with the Presbyterian church and his exposure in the kirk for committing fornication. He married Jean Armour, who already had children by him, in 1788, but his liaisons with other women did not cease. After failing several times as a farmer, Burns became an exciseman in Dumfries in 1791. He died there of heart failure caused by rheumatic fever in 1796, just before the birth of his latest child. He was never free of poverty at any time of his life.

This selection includes many of Burns's best-known lyrics but also celebrates his picture of Scottish rural life, in poems such as 'Poor Maily's Elegy', a touching lament for an old sheep. *Tam o' Shanter* is here in extract, and 'Scots, wha hae'. A brief glossary of Scots words is found on pp. 58–9.

To a Mouse, On turning her up in her Nest, with the Plough, November, 1785

Wee, sleeket, cowran, tim'rous *beastie*,
O, what a panic's in thy breastie!
Thou need na start awa sae hasty,
        Wi' bickering brattle!
I wad be laith to ruin an' chase thee,
        Wi' murd'ring *pattle*!

I'm truly sorry Man's dominion
Has broken Nature's social union,
An' justifies that ill opinion,
        Which makes thee startle,
At me, thy poor, earth-born companion,
        An' *fellow-mortal*!

I doubt na, whyles, but thou may *thieve*;
What then? poor beastie, thou maun live!
A *daimen-icker* in a *thrave*
        'S a sma' request:
I'll get a blessin wi' the lave,
        An' never miss 't!

Thy wee-bit *housie*, too, in ruin!
It's silly wa's the win's are strewin!
An' naething, now, to big a new ane,
        O' foggage green!
An' bleak *December's winds* ensuin,
        Baith snell an' keen!

Thou saw the fields laid bare an' wast,
An' weary *Winter* comin fast,
An' cozie here, beneath the blast,
       Thou thought to dwell,
Till crash! the cruel *coulter* past
        Out thro' thy cell.

That wee-bit heap o' leaves an' stibble,
Has cost thee monie a weary nibble!
Now thou's turn'd out, for a' thy trouble,
       But house or hald,
To thole the Winter's *sleety dribble*,
       An' *cranreuch* cauld!

But Mousie, thou art no thy-lane,
In proving *foresight* may be vain:
The best laid schemes o' *Mice* an' *Men*,
       Gang aft agley,
An' lea'e us nought but grief an' pain,
       For promis'd joy!

Still, thou art blest, compar'd wi' *me*!
The *present* only toucheth thee:
But Och! I *backward* cast my e'e,
       On prospects drear!
An' *forward*, tho' I canna *see*,
       I *guess* an' *fear*!

Burns's Apologia for his Poetry

I am nae *Poet*, in a sense,
But just a *Rhymer* like by chance,
An' hae to Learning nae pretence,
      Yet, what the matter?
Whene'er my Muse does on me glance,
      I jingle at her.

Your Critic-folk may cock their nose,
And say, 'How can you e'er propose,
'You wha ken hardly *verse* frae *prose*,
      'To mak a *sang?*'
But by your leaves, my learned foes,
      Ye're maybe wrang.

What's a' jargon o' your Schools,
Your Latin names for horns an' stools;
If honest Nature made you *fools*,
      What sairs your Grammars?
Ye'd better taen up *spades* and *shools*,
      Or *knappin-hammers*.

A set o' dull, conceited Hashes,
Confuse their brains in *Colledge-classes*!
They *gang* in Stirks, and *come out* Asses,
      Plain truth to speak;
An' syne they think to climb Parnassus
      By dint o' Greek!

Gie me ae spark o' Nature's fire,
That's a' the learning I desire;
Then tho' I drudge thro' dub an' mire
      At pleugh or cart,
My Muse, tho' hamely in attire,
      May touch the heart.

Poor Mailie's Elegy

Lament in rhyme, lament in prose,
Wi' saut tears trickling down your nose;
Our *Bardie*'s fate is at a close,
   Past a' remead!
The last, sad cape-stane of his woes;
   Poor Mailie's dead!

It's no the loss o' warl's gear,
That could sae bitter draw the tear,
Or make our *Bardie*, dowie, wear
   The mourning weed:
He's lost a friend and neebor dear,
   In *Mailie* dead.

Thro' a' the town she trotted by him;
A lang half-mile she could descry him;
Wi' kindly bleat, when she did spy him,
   She ran wi' speed:
A friend mair faithfu' ne'er came nigh him,
   Than *Mailie* dead.

I wat she was a *sheep* o' sense,
An' could behave hersel wi' mense:
I'll say 't, she never brak a fence,
   Thro' thievish greed.
Our *Bardie*, lanely, keeps the spence
   Sin' *Mailie*'s dead.

Or, if he wanders up the howe,
Her living image in *her yowe*,
Comes bleating to him, owre the knowe,
  For bits o' bread;
An' down the briny pearls rowe
  For *Mailie* dead.

She was nae get o' moorlan tips,
Wi' tauted ket, an' hairy hips;
For her forbears were brought in ships,
  Frae 'yont the TWEED:
A bonier *fleesh* ne'er cross'd the clips
  Than *Mailie*'s dead.

Wae worth that man wha first did shape,
That vile, wanchancie thing – *a raep*!
It maks guid fellows girn an' gape,
  Wi' chokin dread;
An' *Robin*'s bonnet wave wi' crape
  For *Mailie* dead.

O, a' ye *Bards* on bonie DOON!
An' wha on AIRE your chanters tune!
Come, join the melancholious croon
  O' *Robins*'s reed!
His heart will never get aboon!
  His *Mailie*'s dead!

From
HOLY WILLIE'S PRAYER

O thou that in the heavens does dwell!
Wha, as it pleases best thysel,
Sends ane to heaven and ten to hell,
      A' for thy glory!
And no for ony gude or ill
      They've done before thee. –

I bless and praise thy matchless might,
When thousands thou has left in night,
That I am here before thy sight,
      For gifts and grace,
A burning and a shining light
      To a' this place. –

O Lord thou kens what zeal I bear,
When drinkers drink, and swearers swear,
And singin' there, and dancin' here
      Wi' great an' sma';
For I am keepet by thy fear,
      Free frae them a'. –

But yet – O Lord – confess I must –
At times I'm fash'd wi' fleshly lust;
And sometimes too, in warldly trust
      Vile Self gets in;
But thou remembers we are dust,
      Defil'd wi' sin. –

O Lord – yestreen – thou kens – wi' Meg –
Thy pardon I sincerely beg!
O may 't ne'er be a living plague,
        To my dishonor!
And I'll ne'er lift a lawless leg
        Again upon her. –

Besides, I farther maun avow,
Wi' Leezie's lass, three times – I trow –
But Lord, that friday I was fou
        When I cam near her;
Or else, thou kens, thy servant true
        Wad never steer her. –

Maybe thou lets this fleshy thorn
Buffet thy servant e'en and morn,
Lest he o'er proud and high should turn,
        That he's sae gifted;
If sae, thy hand maun e'en be borne
        Untill thou lift it. –

But Lord, remember me and mine
Wi' mercies temporal and divine!
That I for grace and gear may shine,
        Excell'd by nane!
And a' the glory shall be thine!
        AMEN! AMEN!

To a Louse, On Seeing one on a Lady's Bonnet at Church

Ha! whare ye gaun, ye crowlan ferlie!
Your impudence protects you sairly:
I canna say but ye strunt rarely,
      Owre *gawze* and *lace*;
Tho' faith, I fear ye dine but sparely,
      On sic a place.

Ye ugly, creepan, blastet wonner,
Detested, shunn'd, by saunt an' sinner,
How daur ye set your fit upon her,
      Sae fine a *Lady!*
Gae somewhere else and seek your dinner,
      On some poor body.

Swith, in some beggar's haffet squattle;
There ye may creep, and sprawl, and sprattle,
Wi' ither kindred, jumping cattle,
      In shoals and nations;
Whare *horn* nor *bane* ne'er daur unsettle,
      Your thick plantations.

Now haud you there, ye're out o' sight,
Below the fatt'rels, snug and tight,
Na faith ye yet! ye'll no be right,
      Till ye've got on it,
The vera tapmost, towrin height
      O' *Miss's bonnet.*

My sooth! right bauld ye set your nose out,
As plump an' gray as onie grozet:
O for some rank, mercurial rozet,
      Or fell, red smeddum,
I'd gie you sic a hearty dose o't,
      Wad dress your droddum!

I wad na been surpriz'd to spy
You on an auld wife's *flainen toy;*
Or aiblins some bit duddie boy,
      On 's *wylecoat;*
But Miss's fine *Lunardi,* fye!
      How daur ye do 't?

O *Jenny* dinna toss your head,
An' set your beauties a' abread!
Ye little ken what cursed speed
      The blastie's makin!
Thae *winks* and *finger-ends,* I dread,
      Are notice takin!

O wad some Pow'r the giftie gie us
To see oursels as others see us!
It wad frae monie a blunder free us
      An' foolish notion:
What airs in dress an' gait wad lea'e us,
      And ev'n Devotion!

Tam Glen

My heart is a breaking, dear Tittie,
  Some counsel unto me come len';
To anger them a' is a pity,
  But what will I do wi' Tam Glen? –

I'm thinking, wi' sic a braw fellow,
  In poortith I might mak a fen':
What care I in riches to wallow,
  If I mauna marry Tam Glen. –

There's Lowrie the laird o' Dumeller,
  'Gude day to you brute' he comes ben:
He brags and he blaws o' his siller,
  But when will he dance like Tam Glen. –

My Minnie does constantly deave me,
  And bids me beware o' young men;
They flatter, she says, to deceive me,
  But wha can think sae o' Tam Glen. –

My Daddie says, gin I'll forsake him,
  He'll gie me gude hunder marks ten:
But, if it's ordain'd I maun take him,
  O wha will I get but Tam Glen?

Yestreen at the Valentines' dealing,
  My heart to my mou gied a sten;
For thrice I drew ane without failing,
  And thrice it was written, Tam Glen. –

The last Halloween I was waukin
  My droukit sark-sleeve, as ye ken;
His likeness cam up the house staukin,
  And the very grey breeks o' Tam Glen!

Come counsel, dear Tittie, don't tarry;
  I'll gie you my bonie black hen,
Gif ye will advise me to Marry
  The lad I lo'e dearly, Tam Glen. –

From
ADDRESS TO A HAGGIS

Fair fa' your honest, sonsie face,
Great chieftain o' the puddin-race!
Aboon them a' ye tak your place,
                    Painch, tripe, or thairm:
Weel are ye wordy of a grace
                    As lang's my arm.

The groaning trencher there ye fill,
Your hurdies like a distant hill,
Your pin wad help to mend a mill
                    In time o' need,
While thro' your pores the dews distil
                    Like amber bead.

Ye Pow'rs, wha mak mankind your care,
And dish them out their bill o' fare,
Auld Scotland wants nae skinking ware,
                    That jaups in luggies;
But, if ye wish her gratefu' prayer,
                    Gie her a Haggis!

'I'm o'er young to marry yet'

I am my mammy's ae bairn,
  Wi' unco folk I weary, Sir,
And lying in a man's bed,
  I'm fley'd it make me irie, Sir.
    I'm o'er young, I'm o'er young,
      I'm o'er young to marry yet;
    I'm o'er young, 'twad be a sin
      To tak me frae my mammy yet.

Hallowmass is come and gane,
  The nights are lang in winter, Sir;
And you an' I in ae bed,
  In trowth, I dare na venture, Sir.
    I'm o'er young etc.

Fu' loud and shill the frosty wind
  Blaws thro' the leafless timmer, Sir;
But if ye come this gate again,
  I'll aulder be gin simmer, Sir.
    I'm o'er young etc.

'Ca' the yowes to the knowes'

Ca' the yowes to the knowes,
   Ca' them whare the heather grows,
Ca' them whare the burnie rowes,
     My bonie Dearie.

Hark, the mavis' evening sang
Sounding Clouden's woods amang;
Then a faulding let us gang,
     My bonie Dearie.
  Ca' the etc.

We'll gae down by Clouden side,
Through the hazels spreading wide
O'er the waves, that sweetly glide
     To the moon sae clearly.
  Ca' the etc.

Yonder Clouden's silent towers,
Where at moonshine midnight hours
O'er the dewy bending flowers
     Fairies dance sae cheary.
  Ca' the etc.

Ghaist nor bogle shalt thou fear;
Thou'rt to Love and Heaven sae dear,
Nocht of Ill may come thee near,
            My bonie Dearie.
      Ca' the etc.

Fair and lovely as thou art,
Thou hast stown my very heart;
I can die – but canna part,
            My bonie Dearie.
      Ca' the etc.

'A red, red rose'

O my Luve's like a red, red rose,
   That's newly sprung in June;
O my Luve's like the melodie
   That's sweetly play'd in tune. –

As fair art thou, my bonie lass,
   So deep in luve am I;
And I will love thee still, my Dear,
   Till a' the seas gang dry. –

Till a' the seas gang dry, my Dear,
   And the rocks melt wi' the sun:
I will love thee still, my Dear,
   While the sands o' life shall run. –

And fare thee weel, my only Luve!
   And fare thee weel, a while!
And I will come again, my Luve,
   Tho' it were ten thousand mile!

The Banks o' Doon

Ye banks and braes o' bonie Doon,
   How can ye bloom sae fresh and fair;
How can ye chant, ye little birds,
   And I sae weary, fu' o' care!
Thou'll break my heart, thou warbling bird,
   That wantons thro' the flowering thorn:
Thou minds me o' departed joys,
   Departed, never to return. –

Oft hae I rov'd by bonie Doon,
   To see the rose and woodbine twine;
And ilka bird sang o' its Luve,
   And fondly sae did I o' mine. –
Wi' lightsome heart I pu'd a rose,
   Fu' sweet upon its thorny tree;
And my fause Luver staw my rose,
   But, ah! he left the thorn wi' me. –

The Primrose

Dost ask me, why I send thee here,
This firstling of the infant year?
Dost ask me, what this primrose shews,
Bepearled thus with morning dews? –

    I must whisper to thy ears,
    The sweets of love are wash'd with tears.

This lovely native of the dale
Thou seest, how languid, pensive, pale:
Thou seest this bending stalk so weak,
That each way yielding doth not break?

    I must tell thee, these reveal,
    The doubts and fears that lovers feel.

'Comin thro' the rye'

Comin thro' the rye, poor body,
   Comin thro' the rye,
She draigl't a' her petticoatie
   Comin thro' the rye.
      Oh Jenny's a' weet, poor body,
       Jenny's seldom dry;
      She draigl't a' her petticoatie
      Comin thro' the rye.

Gin a body meet a body
   Comin' thro' the rye,
Gin a body kiss a body
   Need a body cry.
      Oh Jenny's a' weet, etc.

Gin a body meet a body
   Comin thro' the glen;
Gin a body kiss a body
   Need the warld ken!
      Oh Jenny's a' weet, etc.

'O whistle, and I'll come to ye, my lad'

O whistle, and I'll come to ye, my lad,
O whistle, and I'll come to ye, my lad;
Tho' father, and mother, and a' should gae mad,
    Thy JEANIE will venture wi' ye, my lad.

But warily tent, when ye come to court me,
And come nae unless the back-yett be a-jee;
Syne up the back-style and let naebody see,
    And come as ye were na comin to me –
    And come as ye were na comin to me. –
      O whistle etc.

At kirk, or at market whene'er ye meet me,
Gang by me as tho' that ye car'd nae a flie;
But steal me a blink o' your bonie black e'e,
    Yet look as ye were na lookin at me –
    Yet look as ye were na lookin at me. –
      O whistle etc.

Ay vow and protest that ye care na for me,
And whyles ye may lightly my beauty a wee;
But court nae anither, tho' jokin ye be,
    For fear that she wyle your fancy frae me –
    For fear that she wyle your fancy frae me. –

'John Anderson my jo'

John Anderson my jo, John,
    When we were first acquent;
Your locks were like the raven,
    Your bony brow was brent;
But now your brow is beld, John,
    Your locks are like the snaw;
But blessings on your frosty pow,
    John Anderson my Jo.

John Anderson my jo, John,
    We clamb the hill the gither;
And mony a canty day, John,
    We've had wi' ane anither:
Now we maun totter down, John,
    And hand in hand we'll go;
And sleep the gither at the foot,
    John Anderson my Jo.

Afton Water

Flow gently, sweet Afton, among thy green braes,
Flow gently, I'll sing thee a song in thy praise;
My Mary's asleep by thy murmuring stream,
Flow gently, sweet Afton, disturb not her dream.

Thou stock dove whose echo resounds thro' the glen,
Ye wild whistling blackbirds in yon thorny den,
Thou green crested lapwing thy screaming forbear,
I charge you disturb not my slumbering Fair.

How lofty, sweet Afton, thy neighbouring hills,
Far mark'd with the courses of clear, winding rills;
There daily I wander as noon rises high,
My flocks and my Mary's sweet Cot in my eye.

How pleasant thy banks and green vallies below,
Where wild in the woodlands the primroses blow;
There oft as mild ev'ning weeps over the lea,
The sweet scented birk shades my Mary and me.

Thy chrystal stream, Afton, how lovely it glides,
And winds by the cot where my Mary resides;
How wanton thy waters her snowy feet lave,
As gathering sweet flowerets she stems thy clear wave.

Flow gently, sweet Afton, among thy green braes,
Flow gently, sweet River, the theme of my lays;
My Mary's asleep by thy murmuring stream,
Flow gently, sweet Afton, disturb not her dream.

The Highland Balou

Hee-balou, my sweet, wee Donald,
Picture o' the great Clanronald;
Brawlie kens our wanton Chief
Wha got my wee Highland thief. –

Leeze me on thy bonie craigie,
And thou live, thou'll steal a naigie,
Travel the country thro' and thro',
And bring hame a Carlisle cow. –

Thro' the Lawlands, o'er the Border,
Weel, my babie, may thou furder:
Herry the louns o' the laigh Countrie,
Syne to the Highlands hame to me. –

Robert Bruce's March to Bannockburn –

Scots, wha hae wi' WALLACE bled,
Scots, wham BRUCE has aften led,
Welcome to your gory bed, –
   Or to victorie. –

Now's the day, and now's the hour;
See the front o' battle lour;
See approach proud EDWARD's power,
   Chains and Slaverie. –

Wha will be a traitor-knave?
Wha can fill a coward's grave?
Wha sae base as be a Slave?
   – Let him turn and flie: –

Wha for SCOTLAND's king and law,
Freedom's sword will strongly draw,
FREE-MAN stand, or FREE-MAN fa',
   Let him follow me. –

By Oppression's woes and pains!
By your Sons in servile chains!
We will drain our dearest veins,
   But they *shall* be free!

Lay the proud Usurpers low!
Tyrants fall in every foe!
LIBERTY's in every blow!
   Let us DO – OR DIE!!!

'My heart's in the Highlands'

My heart's in the Highlands, my heart is not
    here;
My heart's in the Highlands a chasing the deer;
Chasing the wild deer, and following the roe;
My heart's in the Highlands, wherever I go. –

Farewell to the Highlands, farewell to the North;
The birth-place of Valour, the country of Worth:
Wherever I wander, wherever I rove,
The hills of the Highlands for ever I love. –

Farewell to the mountains high cover'd with snow;
Farewell to the Straths and green vallies below:
Farewell to the forests and wild-hanging woods;
Farewell to the torrents and loud-pouring floods. –

My heart's in the Highlands, my heart is not here,
My heart's in the Highlands a chasing the deer:
Chasing the wild deer, and following the roe;
My heart's in the Highlands, wherever I go. –

From
ELEGY ON CAPTAIN MATTHEW HENDERSON

Mourn, ilka grove the cushat kens;
Ye hazly shaws and briery dens;
Ye burnies, wimplin down your glens,
   Wi' toddlin din,
Or foaming, strang, wi' hasty stens,
   Frae lin to lin.

Mourn, little harebells o'er the lee;
Ye stately foxgloves fair to see;
Ye woodbines hanging bonnilie,
   In scented bowers;
Ye roses on your thorny tree,
   The first o' flowers.

At dawn, when every grassy blade
Droops with a diamond at his head,
At even, when beans their fragrance shed,
   I' th' rustling gale,
Ye maukins whiddin thro' the glade,
   Come join my wail.

Mourn, ye wee songsters o' the wood;
Ye grouss that crap the heather bud;
Ye curlews calling thro' a clud;
   Ye whistling plover;
And mourn, ye whirring paitrick brood;
   He's gane for ever!

Mourn, sooty coots, and speckled teals;
Ye fisher herons, watching eels;
Ye duck and drake, wi' airy wheels
        Circling the lake:
Ye bitterns, till the quagmire reels,
        Rair for his sake.

Mourn, clamouring craiks at close o' day,
'Mang fields o' flowering claver gay;
And when ye wing your annual way
        Frae our cauld shore,
Tell thae far warlds, wha lies in clay,
        Wham we deplore.

Ye houlets, frae your ivy bower,
In some auld tree, or eldritch tower,
What time the moon, wi' silent glowr,
        Sets up her horn,
Wail thro' the dreary midnight hour
        Till waukrife morn.

TAM O' SHANTER

Warlocks and witches in a dance:
Nae cotillion, brent new frae France,
But hornpipes, jigs, strathspeys, and reels,
Put life and mettle in their heels.
A winnock-bunker in the east,
There sat Auld Nick, in shape o' beast;
A tousie tyke, black, grim, and large,
To gie them music was his charge:
He screw'd the pipes and gart them skirl,
Till roof and rafters a' did dirl.
Coffins stood round, like open presses,
That shaw'd the dead in their last dresses;
And, by some devilish cantraip sleight,
Each in its cauld hand held a light:
By which heroic Tam was able
To note upon the haly table,
A murderer's banes, in gibbet-airns;
Twa span-lang, wee, unchristen'd bairns;
A thief new-cutted frae a rape,
Wi' his last gasp his gab did gape;
Five tomahawks wi' bluid red-rusted;
Five scymitars wi' murder crusted;
A garter which a babe had strangled;
A knife a father's throat had mangled –

Whom his ain son o' life bereft –
The grey-hairs yet stack to the heft;
Wi' mair of horrible and awefu',
Which even to name wad be unlawfu'.
Three Lawyers' tongues, turned inside out,
Wi' lies seamed like a beggar's clout;
Three Priests' hearts, rotten, black as muck,
Lay stinking, vile, in every neuk.

From
ON THE LATE CAPTAIN GROSE'S PEREGRINATIONS THRO' SCOTLAND, COLLECTING THE ANTIQUITIES OF THAT KINGDOM

Hear, Land o' Cakes, and brither Scots,
Frae Maidenkirk to Johny Groats! –
If there's a hole in a' your coats,
⠀⠀⠀⠀⠀I rede you tent it:
A child's amang you, taking notes,
⠀⠀⠀⠀⠀And, faith, he'll prent it.

If in your bounds ye chance to light
Upon a fine, fat, fodgel wight,
O' stature short, but genius bright,
⠀⠀⠀⠀⠀That's he, mark weel –
And wow! he has an unco slight
⠀⠀⠀⠀⠀O' cauk and keel.

By some auld, houlet-haunted, biggin,
Or kirk deserted by its riggin,
It's ten to ane ye'll find him snug in
⠀⠀⠀⠀⠀Some eldritch part,
Wi' deils, they say, Lord safe 's! colleaguin
⠀⠀⠀⠀⠀At some black art. –

He has a fouth o' auld nick-nackets:
Rusty airn caps and jinglin jackets,
Wad haud the Lothians three in tackets,
        A towmont gude;
And parritch-pats, and auld saut-backets,
        Before the Flood.

Of Eve's first fire he has a cinder;
Auld Tubalcain's fire-shool and fender;
That which distinguished the gender
        O' Balaam's ass;
A broom-stick o' the witch of Endor,
        Weel shod wi' brass.

Forbye, he'll shape you aff fu' gleg
The cut of Adam's philibeg;
The knife that nicket Abel's craig
        He'll prove you fully,
It was a faulding jocteleg,
        Or lang-kail gullie. –

But wad ye see him in his glee,
For meikle glee and fun has he,
Then set him down, and twa or three
        Gude fellows wi' him;
And *port, O port!* shine thou a wee,
        And THEN ye'll see him!

Epitaph on John Dove, Innkeeper, Mauchline

Here lies Johnny Pidgeon,
What was his religion,
Whae'er desires to ken,
To some other warl
Maun follow the carl,
For here Johnny Pidgeon had nane.

Strong ale was ablution,
Small beer persecution,
A dram was *memento mori*;
But a full flowing bowl,
Was the saving his soul,
And Port was celestial glory.

Epitaph on a Wag in Mauchline

Lament 'im Mauchline husbands a',
    He aften did assist ye;
For had ye staid whole weeks awa'
    Your wives they ne'er had miss'd ye.

Ye Mauchline bairns as on ye pass,
    To school in bands thegither,
O tread ye lightly on his grass,
    Perhaps he was your father.

Epitaph on a Schoolmaster in Cleish Parish, Fifeshire

Here lie Willie Michie's banes,
    O Satan, when ye tak him,
Gie him the schulin' o' your weans;
    For clever Deils he'll mak 'em!

GLOSSARY

The eighteenth-century Lowland Scots in which Burns wrote so many of his finest poems is not especially difficult for modern non-Scots speakers to understand, its hurdles being often a matter of spelling. To this end, the following short glossary confines itself to matters of vocabulary – that is, Scots words which are peculiar to Scotland or which do not signify the same thing that they do in standard English. Readers are, however, urged to pronounce Burns's poems aloud, chiefly to secure their expert and original metrical finesse.

ablins, aiblins, perhaps
aboon, up, above, over
ae, ane, one, only
agley, awry
airn, iron
amaist, almost
balou, lullaby
ben, indoors, inner room
bestead, placed, circumstanced
biggin, building, cottage
birk, birch tree
birkie, lively, spry fellow
bogle, ghost, spirit, spectre
brae, high ground, river bank
brattle, clatter, noise, hurry
braw, brawlie, handsome, splendid, admirably
breeks, trousers, breeches
cantraip, magic
canty, lively, cheerfully
coof, fool, clown, lout
coulter, hoe, garden or farm implement
craig, cragie, neck, throat, gullet
cranreuch, hoar-frost
crowlan, creeping
cushat, wood-pigeon
cutty, short

daimin-icker, occasional ear of corn
deave, deafen
dirl, ring
dizzen, dozen, hank of spun thread
dowie, sad, miserable, melancholy
draigl't, bedraggled
droddum, backside
droukit, drenched, soaked
dub, pool, mud, stagnant, muddy
eldritch, uncanny, unearthly
fash, trouble, bother
fatt'rels, ribbon-ends
ferlie, marvel, wonder
fier, hearty, sound
flainen, flannel
fley'd, terrified, frightened
flie, fly; also valueless
fodgel, plump, good-humoured
fou, full, drunk; also emphatic
gab, mouth
gear, possessions, property, money, liquor, etc.
get, offspring, brat
gleg, quick, lively, smart
grozet, gooseberry
gullie, large knife
ha'et, have it
haffet, temple, hair lock on same

herry, harry, plunder

hoddin, cloth woven from black and white wool

howe, hollow, valley, glen

hurdies, backside, buttocks

ilk, ilka, each, every

irie, eerie

jad, mare (whence hussy, wench, etc.)

jaup, splash

jocteleg, clasp-knife

kail, vegetable of cabbage family, provender (lang-kail, Scotch kail)

ket, matted, hairy fleece of wool

knappin-hammer, hammer for breaking stones

knowe, mound, hillock

lane, lonely, solitary

lave, rest, remainder, others

lin(n), waterfall, cataract

luggies, porringers

maist, almost

maukin, hare, buck-hare

mavis, thrush

meikle, great, plentiful, much

mense, sense, decorum, moderation, tact

naig, naigie, small horse

painch, paunch

paitrick, partridge

parritch-pat, porridge-pot

pattle, small spade used to clean a plough

philibeg, kilt

poortith, poverty

pow, head

press, cupboard

raep, rape, rope

rowe, roll, wrap

rozet, resin

run-deil, complete, thorough-going devil

sair, serve, treat, satisfy; or sore, sorry, hard, harsh

sark, shirt, chemise, shift (as in 'cutty sark')

scroggie, covered with stunted bushes

sic, such

skinking, watery

skirl, squeal

smeddum, powder used in medicine

snell, keen, bitter

sonsie, jolly

sowther, solder, repair

spence, parlour, inner room

squattle, squat, nestle down

staukin, stalking, moving stealthily

sten, leap, bound

strunt, move with assurance, stalk (as noun, liquor)

syne, then, since ('lang syne', long since, long ago)

tacket, hobnail for boots

tent, heed, care, attend

thairm, small guts

thole, endure, suffer

thrave, measure of corn or straw

tint, lost

tirled, uncovered, unthatched; or unleased (latch)

toddlan, toddlin, walking unsteadily, toddling

towmont, twelve months, a year

tyke, dog, cur, mongrel

unco, odd, strange

wae, woe

wanchancie, dangerous, unlucky

waukin, awake, sleepless

waukrife, wakeful, vigilant

wha, wham, who, whom

whiddin, moving nimbly

winnock-bunker, window-seat

wonner, wonder, marvel

yestreen, yesterday evening

yett, gate

yowe, ewe

SOURCES OF THE EXTRACTS

Epistle to J. Lapraik, stanzas 9, 10, 11, 12, 13.
Holy Willie's Prayer, stanzas 1, 2, 6, 7, 8, 9, 10, 17.
Address to a Haggis, stanzas 1, 2, 8.
Elegy on Captain Matthew Henderson, stanzas 4 to 10.
Tam o' Shanter, lines 125 to 146.
On the Late Captain Gross's Pereginations, stanzas 1, 2, 3, 6, 7, 8, 9.

NOTES ON THE PICTURES

p.6   *Robert Burns, c.* 1828, a posthumous portrait by Alexander Nasmyth (1758–1840). Scottish National Portrait Gallery, Edinburgh.

p.14   *An Autumn Morning,* 1897, by Sir George Clausen (1852–1944). Fine Art Society, London.

p.19   *The Rescue* by Richard Ansdell (1815–85). Malcolm Innes Gallery, London.

p.22   *The Sleeping Congregation,* 1736, by William Hogarth (1697–1764). The Mansell Collection, London.

p.27   *Robert Burns and Highland Mary* by James Archer (1823–1904). Roy Miles Fine Paintings, London.

p.31   *A Scottish Fair* (detail) by John Phillip (1817–67). Towneley Hall Art Gallery and Museum, Burnley.

p.35   *The Dawn of Love,* 1846, by Thomas Brooks (1818–91). Victoria and Albert Museum, London.

p.39   *The Harvest* (detail) by Hugh Cameron (1835–1918). Private collection.

p.43   *A Highland River Landscape* (detail) by Daniel Sherrin (fl.1895–1915). Christopher Wood Gallery, London.

p.47   *Monarch of the Glen, c.* 1851, by Sir Edwin Landseer (1802–73). John Dewar and Sons Ltd, London.

p.51   *Tam O' Shanter (The Legend of the Cutty Sark),* by unknown artist. This painting hangs in the *Cutty Sark,* Greenwich.

p.54   *Captain Francis Grose* by unknown artist. Scottish National Portrait Gallery, Edinburgh.

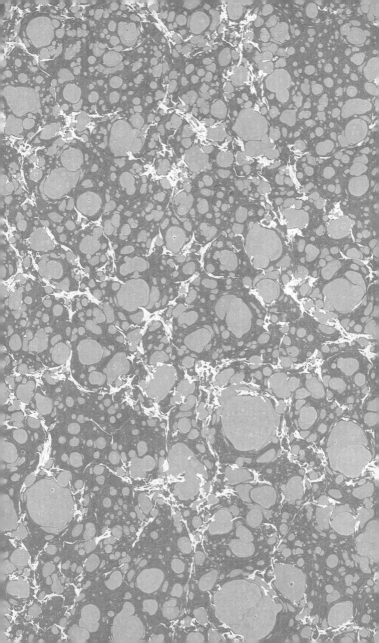